Keeping Couponing Real

Keeping Couponing Real

Couponing for those who don't have time to coupon

J. Kelly Charles

**Book One in the
"Lunch Break Reading" Series**

For my mother
Who taught me all I know

I don't have time for that

Time for what?

Does it matter? I bet you could fill in that blank with almost anything...

"I don't have time to exercise."

"I don't have time to cook every day."

"I need to clean out the garage but I don't have time."

"I wish I had more time to spend with my family."

It's an endless list, isn't it? But despite the fact that a day will always consist of 24 hours, don't we still tend to hope that *someday* we will find time for all those things on our to-do list?

Thus the premise behind many a New Year's Resolution...

"I will find time to exercise."

"I will cook more at home and eat out less."

"I will clean out the garage."

And "I will spend more time with my family."

Because somehow we just know that things will change. That the plates that are our hectic schedules will clear, or that we will find some better way of organizing our days' activities, resulting in just a little more time for things we *want* to do rather than the same old *have* to do list.

Unfortunately, rarely is our wish granted. Short of an unwanted event such as illness or the loss of a job, spare time on any sort of consistent basis eludes most of us. Which is why we hesitate to commit to projects that we know will require just that - especially when there's already a waiting list of activities ready to fill every moment.

"I don't have time for that" is the number one reason I hear when it comes to why many don't maximize the use of coupons. They've perhaps seen some of us on television talking about the time and effort it takes - hearing stories of 20, 30, even 40 hours or more spent weekly clipping coupons, organizing, and shopping. Is it any wonder why so many are intimidated by the very thought of taking on anything that would require that kind of time?

To be sure, I don't have that kind of time either. As a working mom, I join millions of busy parents who do well just to keep the house picked up and some sort of dinner on the table in between a full time job and three teenagers, all with their own itineraries to manage. And by "working", I acknowledge that a stay-at-home parent arguably works just as hard as one with a secular job outside the home!

Yes, regardless of our circumstances, the one common thread that runs through most of our lives is simply a lack of as much spare time as we'd wish.

I'm here to tell you... I have found a way to save thousands on household expenses. *Thousands!* And on the same tight schedule that you and I are accustomed to. In fact, I dare say that time is not even a component in the savings equation. It's about changing the way you *think* when you shop.

So what is the secret? Are coupons the answer? They're part of it, but really they're just the icing on the cake - like bonus savings on top of an already-smart spending strategy. You must first understand the concepts of what I call "Smart Shopping". This is not in complicated in the least, just perhaps a little different than what most are used to. But it takes no more time out of your schedule, no more planning, no more work even than what you already do. Once you realize the first taste of significant savings, you'll wonder how you ever shopped any other way.

Notice that this isn't a very thick book... That's because I don't need lots of pages to explain the concepts of Smart Shopping. Its simplicity is what makes it so great!

An eye-opener

Yet again, the hours of the day have been stolen away from us and we find it nearing dinnertime with no dinner in the making. So much for our plan to cook a nice, well-rounded meal just once this week. With a slight wince of guilt, we preheat the oven for yet another frozen pizza, alleviating a bit of the guilt by reasoning that wasn't it for just such an occasion that we bought the frozen pizzas in the first place?

Unwrapping the $6.99 dinner to top with a bit of fresh mozzarella and basil so it doesn't seem quite so packaged, we further rationalize our decision. In lieu of the originally planned well-rounded meal, the alternative would be to head out to eat where, for a family of 4, the bill could easily exceed $40. Why, add to our current pizza a $3.69 bag of pre-packaged salad and a $2.99 package of garlic bread and Voila! We've *saved* money! Right? A little more content with ourselves, we vow to save the nice dinner for another day. When we have more time.

While many of us would love to feed our families the way our mothers and grandmothers fed theirs, most often what stands in the way is that same old lack of time. We either don't have time to do the actual cooking, have not had time to learn how, or don't feel we have time to properly grocery shop. It's why most of us eat out, settle for the above-described meal, or at best make a quick run to the store on the way home to "grab something for dinner". In any case, we often spend a large portion of our income on, well, food. And often not great food at that.

Most would be surprised to know how much they actually spend on food. Again, if we had all the time in the world to ponder such things, we might sit down weekly and examine every expenditure, keep running totals and note room for improvement. But for those of us who live in the real world, as long as the bills are paid on time and there's something to eat at mealtime we figure we've done okay.

Years ago I created a spreadsheet for our family finances*. While I hated math in school, I was pretty good at it and later found that, despite my 11th grade prediction, it is actually useful in "real life". It bothered me that I didn't know where every penny was spent, that our paychecks were direct deposited into an account from which we withdrew throughout the month until the well got low and we would stop spending until it was refilled.

I clearly remember the first tally of monthly expenses, and the resulting gasp of horror upon realizing that yes, we spent *that* much eating out! As shocking as it was, however, it only prompted half-hearted action. A few more dinners at home but no significant savings.

Until hardship forced our hand. Fuel prices topped $4.00/gallon, and with over 250 miles commuted daily between my husband and myself just to get back and forth to work, something had to give! Our bank account just wasn't equipped to accommodate the $1200+ monthly fuel bill, but what could we do? We had to work, and we had to drive to get there. There had to be somewhere we could cut.

I recalled that my mother and grandmother had faithfully clipped coupons throughout my childhood. Now, my mother is, in my humble and completely unbiased but correct opinion, the most frugal person on the planet. With an uncanny ability to stretch every penny into a dime and every dime into a dollar, I still find it hard to believe that she doesn't have a money tree hidden somewhere in a closet. She always was good with a garden, so I'm sure if such a thing exists she'd be the one to cultivate it!

But back to my point - I used to wonder why she and Granny bothered with coupons when their amounts seemed so small. I'd always tried to be a frugal shopper, but mainly only used coupons when it was convenient or for high dollar amounts. Given the circumstances we were presented with, the adage that "every penny counts" took on a whole new meaning and I decided to see what I could do with some serious couponage.

So I clipped inserts from a couple Sunday papers. Without any real plan, I took my coupons proudly to the grocery store, ready to save. Oh how I wish I'd had a guidebook like this one back then!

Couponage: The act or process of using coupons.

In addition to math, I also have a talent for making up words...

After the first trip to the store, I was hooked. I saved very little, really, but I was immediately addicted to the savings, and I challenged myself to do better. Each subsequent trip was my own contest - how well could I do this time?

I'm going to fast-forward to the punch line. Not to spoil the ending as much as to inspire you to commit to what you're reading... Recall my shock upon realizing how much we were spending on food? Between groceries and restaurants, that number was consistently between $1200-1300/month. Was.

After you pick up your jaw, realize this... That number has dropped to around $200/month. Yep, $200. For a family of 5 that includes a teenage boy who can eat his weight in bacon for breakfast alone.

Could *you* use an extra $1000 in your pocket each month?

Read on.

Changing the way you think

The whole couponing fad has everyone thinking coupons are the key to saving. Just clip coupons, you'll save thousands! However, there's a reason I simply call them the icing and not the cake itself. Before you can experience real savings, you have to change your approach to shopping. What do I mean?

First consider the Old Way. I give it a title for identification purposes, because once you define your own Old Way you can avoid it. A typical Old Way might look like this...

Your grocery shopping list consists of items you need for the week, and you likely shop at the store that is either most convenient or that you feel will have the best prices. Once in the store, you go about the task of checking off the list.

Now, frugal shopper that you are, you're not going to just toss items in the cart indiscriminately. No,

11

you're after a bargain! You compare prices, sizes, and brands, confident that each selected item is the best value. Then comes a nice surprise - one of your list items is on sale! Woo hoo! Proud of this unexpected bargain, you look for more bright yellow sale tags. Oh look, another! And you're hungry, so if you're anything like me the cart isn't making it through the bakery without a package of cheese danishes. Not on the list, but one more item won't hurt. Besides, you're saving on those sale items! You reach checkout, proud that at least a portion of your list will be less than retail.

Old Way:

Buying what you need and hoping for a good sale price

The fault in this logic is that we forget one thing... the store placed these items on sale because they *wanted* us to buy them. Indeed they budget for just such a transaction as ours. An examination of every other checkout lane might reveal that a similar percentage of those transactions are also sale items. Did we really do anything special? Regardless of what items were on our list, isn't it likely that a portion of them would have been on sale?

Remember that in any competitive marketplace, making you feel good about your purchase is the ultimate goal. Perception is not always reality, but we rarely recognize the difference. If we perceive that we got a good deal, we will shop again. Successful marketing!

So what's wrong with the Old Way? Nothing, actually, except that you'll never really save more than 25-30% on your groceries, even with coupons.

Which leads us to the New Way.

Consider: What if everything you ever purchased was on sale? Instead of lucking up on a few sale items, you could purchase nothing *but* sale items. Imagine the savings! And you haven't even clipped the first coupon. (Yet. We'll get to that in a minute.)

Obviously the chances of every item we need being on sale are slim and none. As much as I may be loyal to my local grocery store, they're just not going to tailor their weekly sale to my

> **New Way:**
>
> Buy what's on sale, and buy enough to last until the next great sale

needs. So my list has to conform to their sale. The list is no longer what we *need*, but what's *on sale*.

That's well and good, you say, but I need things this week that just aren't on sale. What to do? The transition from "need" to "sale" list is a short process, but one that you can easily start now. This week. And it brings us to the first and perhaps most important concept of Smart Shopping:

Buy at rock-bottom price, and buy enough to last until the next rock-bottom price.

Your list this week will have to consist of what you need because, well, you need it. But while shopping, also take note of great prices on items you will *use,* though maybe not urgently needed just yet.

> **Rock-Bottom Price:**
>
> The price at which you can comfortably tell yourself, "I'm probably not going to find it any cheaper."

So you don't need peanut butter this week, but it's on sale for a great price. And your family eats its fair share of peanut butter. What are the chances it will be on sale when you do need it? Why not buy now, and buy enough to last awhile? We're not talking Doomsday preparation here... by "awhile" I simply mean long enough to last until you're likely to find another great price. And just like that, you'll never pay full price for peanut butter again.

As you take advantage of these great bargains week after week, you'll see your "needs" list dwindle to almost nothing, allowing for the aforementioned cart full of little else than great sale items.

Depending on your family's eating habits and your store's sale cycles, you might count on about two months to fully transition from the "needs list" to the "sale list".

Logically, your initial savings will be reflected more as a percentage than a dollar amount, given the purchase of extra sale items. However, in just a few short weeks you'll begin to notice a drastic difference in your weekly spending.

Wonderful! We're saving money! The concept itself is simple, but the application causes many to throw their hands up in frustration. Why? Because once you have changed the way you think when you shop, always in search of rock-bottom pricing, it's easy to mistake "always buy on sale" for "can't miss a sale". And "can't miss a sale" will drive you nuts, not to mention take away all the time that you already don't have.

What's the key to finding the things you need on sale without hours of planning and running all over town? Again, I wish I'd had this guidebook back when I first asked myself that question!

> Don't mistake
> "Buy on Sale" for
> "Can't Miss a Sale"

Time = Money

We've already established that if this coupon thing takes too much of our time, we're out. Fortunately, that doesn't have to be an issue. To understand why not, it helps to first understand the misconception that couponing is practically a full time job.

I live in a fairly rural area, but we southerners like to eat. Despite the rurality, there are no less than 8 grocery stores nearby. Add to that 2 super centers and countless drug and bargain stores, and we're talking a lot of stores to shop. Each with its own policy and sale cycle, suddenly I have quite a large stack of papers to scour and lists to make. I'm already tired just thinking about such a task, and the idea that I have to do this weekly? Double Ugh!

But it's necessary, right? I mean, isn't the whole idea to catch the best sales?

Not exactly. Not if you want to keep your sanity, anyway. On a given week, it's likely that there will be great deals in at least 2 of the grocery stores, a couple drug stores, and the super center. If I were to narrow it down to just these, that's 5 shopping lists, 5 trips into the store, 5 times I have to match up coupons to sale items, 5 checkouts... You get the point. And what if a store is out of an item, which will almost surely happen in at least one store? That's a rain check, and yet another trip back.

Who has time for all that? But if you subscribe to any coupon blogs or Facebook fan pages (even mine), you will be presented with all of these great deals and may feel a sense of obligation to snag every one. Free toothbrushes at Walgreens this week! Free shampoo on clearance at CVS, but hurry or they'll run out! Razors are a money-maker at Walmart, and they just restocked!

All that running around for just a handful of items at each stop. I don't have to remind you of the cost of fuel. And what is your time worth?

Here's where I wish I'd had this advice a long time ago, because I tried deal-chasing. It was positively maddening, and consumed way too much of my schedule to be practical.

I decided that I'd just stick to my one main grocery store and shop nowhere else. I chose to ignore the possibility of a great price elsewhere and to just take advantage of whatever sale my main store had for the week. For me, the peace of mind was worth missing an occasional freebie.

Now here came the surprise...

I didn't miss anything! I was still able to get everything our family can use, at great prices, and didn't spend any more than if I'd run all over town!

I explained all of that to say this: Saving thousands on your groceries really does boil down to just one thing - changing the way you *think* when you shop. And *thinking* doesn't take any extra time. You were going to the store anyway, you've just rearranged what goes into the cart and when.

So here's your strategy:
Select a grocery store that is convenient to you but that also has the best coupon policy. Have one in mind? Do they carry fresh meat and produce? Frozen and refrigerated goods? Household supplies and cleaners? Pharmaceutical goods? Personal care items? Of course they do. And don't all of these items go on sale at some point? Yep again.

So why not just make that your primary shopping destination? Eventually everything you use will have its spot in the sale rotation, and when it does, buy it! Don't worry that you may have missed free toothpaste across town. You'll catch the same deal at your own store at some point.

Let's be realistic - I am not suggesting that you never step foot in another store. What I am saying is that once you are accustomed to paying rock bottom prices, it's easy to feel a twinge of guilt at passing one up. And face it, the high of getting something for free or stupid cheap is more than a little addictive. We want to experience it again and again. But shopping in multiple stores should be the *exception*, not the rule.

Obviously this one-store plan saves the time and cost involved in driving all over town, but it has other time-saving advantages as well.

Fast shopping...

If you're primarily in the same store regularly, you know it like the back of your hand. Canned soup? Aisle 4. Laundry detergent, aisle 8. Popcorn, aisle 13. You can breeze through your shopping list in no time.

Staying organized...

There's another whole section devoted to organization, but it bears mentioning here because the whole one-store routine really assists with this. Shopping in one main store allows you to organize your binder by aisle and make your list in similar fashion.

Easy checkout...

We know that couponing is smart, but unfortunately the rest of the world has not yet received that memo. This includes the majority of cashiers you will encounter. It doesn't seem like much to ask for a cashier to know the coupon policy of the store where they're employed, but sadly many just don't have a clue. There's that moment of uncertainty when you approach the register... What lane do I choose? Which cashier looks to be the most coupon-friendly? What if I'm wrong?

Almost as frustrating as a cashier who knows nothing about coupons is the one who is quite diligent about her job and feels it her duty to carefully inspect each coupon, pulling items from your already-bagged purchase to confirm their validity. It's not unusual to feel treated like a criminal for trying to save money. Inevitably the cashier on either extreme will find at least one coupon that is completely unacceptable, then ignore your logical explanation as to why it is indeed valid. Obviously you wouldn't know, since you don't work there.

It is incredibly uncomfortable (and usually futile anyway) to be in a position of telling an employee how to do their own job. You may politely ask for a manger, but the employee has likely been trained by this very manager and often he or she is little more educated on coupons than the cashier. Meanwhile you apologize to the customers behind you in line, but can sense their aggravation at having to wait. And there's rarely a good outcome - the manager either upholds the coupon refusal or agrees to accept but only as a "customer service", as if to validate that you are indeed trying to pull something but they're going to overlook it just this once.

Your being a regular in the same store helps minimize the chances of that whole scenario. You get to know the cashiers, and they you. You're more likely to receive the benefit of the doubt when the register beeps its rejection at your coupon, and the two of you can laugh it off as a silly computer glitch.

Knowing that the actual process of shopping doesn't have to be tedious nor consume any more of your precious time is surely a relief. But with the sales changing weekly, even within your main stores, how is one to know what is the proper "rock-bottom price", prompting stock purchase?

Rock bottom pricing

What defines "rock-bottom pricing"? In a nutshell, it's the lowest price you're likely to find for the foreseeable future.

You are likely aware of the general prices of items that your family uses on a regular basis. Therefore, you can spot when that price is significantly less than normal.

Keeping an eye on the regular prices of the items you use will make the great sale prices obvious to you. But to be sure, here are a few common tricks used by grocery stores to make you *think* you've found a great price:

- **Sale tags:** While a great sale will certainly be marked by a tag, a sale tag does not necessarily indicate a great price.

- **End cap items:** The ends of the aisles, called "end caps" are some of the most valuable real estate in the store. Because of this, stores often place items here that they want to push, usually accompanied by a big sale sign. A marketing ploy designed to create the illusion of a great deal. Because these items are pulled away from their usual aisle space, it's not as convenient to comparison-shop and easier to assume the price is great.

- **Closeouts:** Just the word "closeout" is exciting! It creates the perception of urgency - "get it now before it's gone", and the assumption again is that it must be a deal. While closeouts can often indeed be a great price, that's not necessarily the case. A closeout price may be little less than regular price, and some stores will not accept coupons on closeout items. Be sure it's a good price, and know your store's coupon policy on these items.

- **Bigger isn't always better:** A common misconception is that the larger size is the better value. Not necessarily, particularly if you have coupons. Do the cost-per-unit math, including your coupon amount. You may find that the small or medium sized packages are the best value.

- **Deals in Multiples:** A "10 for $10" sale may simply mean $1 each. Obviously the store would prefer you buy 10 (hence the wording), but it may not be necessary to get the sale price. The same with "Buy 1 Get 1 Free" (otherwise known as BOGO) deals - often one item will ring up half price, so no need to buy in sets of 2.

Now that you've identified a great sale price (what you might call the "cake"), it's time to add the "icing" - coupons! It is this equation that will result in your drastic savings:

Great Sale + Coupon = Rock Bottom Price

Both a sale and a coupon will result in savings, but it's the combination of the two that result in the *huge* savings that we're after. Here's an example:

You have a coupon for $.50 off Lipton tea. Being that sweet tea is its own food group in our house, I'm quite familiar with this example. Particularly during the summer, we can easily go through a gallon of the stuff each day!

So anyway, the coupon. Let's say the Lipton is priced $3.69/box. Your $.50 coupon brings it down to $3.19, or if you're lucky enough to shop at a store that doubles, $2.69.

Consider:
$2.69 is a not-so-great sale price, as it's not unusual for the tea to be on sale for considerably less. Your use of a coupon on the regular price resulted in little more than an okay sale price. But what if the tea were part of a BOGO sale. At 2 for $3.69, your price is already down to $1.85 and $1.84. Now use the coupon on top of the sale, and you've got yourself a rock bottom price! If taken at

face value, the coupon brings the tea down to $1.35, or a 63% savings vs. regular price. If doubled, the final price becomes $.85, a 77% savings. Now those are the numbers we are after!

At such a great price, why would you not buy enough to last until you're likely to find a similar great price again? Depending on shelf life and your consumption rate, this might be anywhere from 1-2 items to a 6-month supply or more. A super good deal (like, FREE!) on an item with a long shelf life (like cleaners) might result in your purchasing even more.

Thus your stockpile is born. We'll discuss stockpiling a bit more later on, but since we opened the topic of coupons let's continue with that...

Great sale + coupon = rock bottom price

Rock bottom price = stockpile purchase

The fun part... Coupons!

Couponing has become quite a trend. You've seen it on television, may have even seen me on there a few times, handing over hundreds - even thousands - of dollars in coupons and walking out of the store with several full carts, having paid only a few cents. Or better yet, getting money back. All because of coupons!

Picking up on the fad, it seems that every other shopping cart in the grocery store now has a binder sitting properly in the child seat, or at the very least the mom behind the wheels has a handful of coupons paper-clipped to her shopping list, armed to save!

The savings create an attractive picture, and all too often a well-intentioned couponer will embark on this money-saving venture, only to throw in the towel shortly after, unhappy with her savings percentage and discouraged that it just seems too hard. Such persons often ask me, "what's the secret?"

There is indeed a secret, but not because any of us are trying to keep it to ourselves. It's simply that coupons alone won't result in massive savings, as you've already learned here. It's the formula of sale price + coupon + stockpile that works, and most leave out at least one element.

We've covered the sale price part of the equation - not only by definition but from an angle that will not frustrate your schedule. Now to discuss the coupon bit, with the same considerations, and starting with the basics.

Get the coupons...

It really does no good to discuss what to do with coupons if you don't have any. Not to sound redundant, but you'd be amazed how many folks I have tried to help, week after week talking them through what to do, how to organize, etc. I may volunteer to go shopping with them, then ask where their coupons are. I get this sheepish look as they make excuses for how they've forgotten to get a paper the last few Sundays, but pull out pages of coupons that they printed out the night before.

Now, I am arguably the single most forgetful person I know, so I really can't fault the forgetting thing. Unfortunately my daughter has inherited this lovely trait from me, so I am teaching her how to work around it. I know I'm forgetful, so I keep notes and lists. And a spreadsheet for everything. The Sunday paper is no different; if left to my memory to pick one up weekly I'd probably succeed a couple times a month.

Knowing how slippery my mind is, I leave nothing to it and I simply subscribe to the Sunday-only edition of the paper. It's often cheaper than news stand price and someone brings it to *you!*

Most newspapers will allow concurrent multiple subscriptions. You may opt for a couple of papers, but several subscriptions is not the answer. It invites delivery issues, and you'll almost surely be on the phone many Monday mornings obtaining credit for at least one undelivered copy. Not to mention that there will be weeks when the inserts just aren't great, yet you'll have paid for them anyway.

Subscription tips:

- Subscribe to Sunday-only

- Ask for an introductory rate, often less than newsstand

- Pay attention to when your rate expires and negotiate

I have found that inserts aren't hard to come by. I ask friends, family, and coworkers to save inserts they don't intend to use. You'll be surprised how many people just throw them away (after all, you used to do the same thing). Now they'll throw them your way!

Inserts can be obtained fairly cheaply online from a number of sources. While it is not legal to buy/sell coupons, it is perfectly legal to pay someone for their time and effort to obtain, sort, clip, and distribute them. There are even subscription services available, such as the one at www.couponinsertservice.com, which will mail inserts to you automatically each week.

You might ask your paper carrier if they have extra papers or inserts at the end of their route. Some are required to recycle these, but some (particularly smaller papers) end up with extras that they may not mind passing along to you.

I started bringing my unwanted coupons in to work and placing in a designated basket in the break room, and asked others to do the same. Between us all, there is usually quite a stack of coupons to share. Monday mornings are fun again! Well, almost.

If you have trouble finding coupons for a particular item or brand that you love, try calling the manufacturer. Most products have a toll-free number right on the packaging. I personally have a list of all the companies in my pantry**, and make a few calls each week to and from my work commute. It takes no extra time, and simply praising the company for their product or asking where to find coupons often results in their sending them. Occasionally I get surprised with coupons for free product!

The Internet is also a great resource for printing coupons. However, this useful tool can be a little overwhelming. Again, in the interest of keeping things simple, bearing in mind a few pointers when printing online will make your couponing life easier:

- Don't use search engines to search for printable coupons. The majority of the results will be expired or wild goose chases.

- Stick to one or two sites (like mine, www.workingmomcoupons.com), and use the links on those sites to find your printables. The main printable coupon sites will be linked here anyway, and usually some other great printables that may otherwise have taken you hours to round up on your own.

- Use social media to your benefit. Most great sites (including mine) have Facebook fan pages and Twitter accounts, and any other popular social media channel. Being a fan allows you to receive notice each time new printables and deals are posted, saving you the trouble of checking in.

- Print only what you will use. Don't let your savings be offset by the printer ink used to print unnecessary coupons!

You know how moms have that extra sense that tells us what our kids are up to? Similarly, as a couponer you will develop "coupon radar" – a sense that ensures you will notice coupons everywhere you go! For instance...

Coupons can often be found directly on products. Those words "Save Now!" on a peelie coupon will practically give you whiplash as you walk by! Tearpads are often strategically placed near items to encourage impulse buys. Blinkies stand out from shelves dispensing coupons one at a time for nearby products. Your newly found coupon radar will alert you to coupons everywhere!

- **Peelies**: Coupons found directly on products, usually requiring you to peel it off

- **Tearpads**: Pads of coupons from which you can tear as needed

- **Blinkies**: An electronic coupon dispenser, often on a timer to dispense one coupon at a time.

Which leads me off track in the discussion for just a moment. We'll get back to the point, but the subject of in-store coupons is so controversial that I can't resist sharing my .02 worth.

The hotly-debated question is: should one take peelies or coupons from tearpads or blinkies if not buying that product that day? And if so, what is the "acceptable" number of coupons to take?

Like with most things, everyone has an opinion. While the following is only my opinion, it is at least based on some logic.

Consider: Manufacturer coupons, regardless of where they are obtained, are provided by the manufacturers to you, the consumer, as an incentive to purchase their products. Often, in-store coupons are placed on or near items by company reps who are responsible for merchandising their brands within the store. Their goal is obviously to increase sales.

With that knowledge, I feel that it is perfectly acceptable to take such coupons, as long as it is with the intention of actually purchasing the product. Now, *when* I purchase it will be determined by a good sale price, which may or not be today, but if I put the coupon to good use then I feel no harm is done.

Logically, this leads to the question of *how many* coupons to take. I consider this logic to be similar to that of shelf-clearing. Just use common sense and be considerate of other shoppers. I can't tell you how many is too many, but your common sense should tell you that to take every coupon from a well-stocked shelf is just plain rude!

Coupons are everywhere!

Sunday newspapers   Print online   Trade

Online printables   Subscription services

Ask!   In-Store   On products

Organize the coupons...

Now you have coupons in hand, what to do? If you've ever been in a checkout lane behind a disorganized couponer, you don't have to be told the value of organization.

Next to "How do you find the time?", the question I probably get more than any other is "How do you stay organized?" This one always makes me laugh, because I would argue that I am the single most *disorganized* person I know. I am always making to-do lists, to no avail because I simply lose them. I set alarms on my phone and then forget what I set them for. The neighbor calls asking for a cup of sugar and I walk over empty-handed. It's quite sad, really.

So how on earth do I manage to organize my shopping, coupons, and lists to accomplish the massive savings that I do? I discovered that it wasn't nearly as difficult as I would have thought. The first, and probably most important essential to organization is The Binder.

The Binder

At first I resisted The Binder. An accordion file will work just fine, I thought. Properly labeled and packed to the point that the rubber band holding it closed was stretched out of shape and useless, I was determined that it was sufficient. However, after missing far too many deals because I couldn't find that coupon that I knew was in there somewhere, and a couple times dropping the whole darn thing in the store and I had to admit that there surely is a better system. I succumbed to the idea, and of course now wonder how I ever managed without it.

There sat my nifty new binder and stack of coupons. Where to start? How to arrange it? I ponder this at length, actually. There are a number of ways to organize a binder, but at first none quite met my standards for user-friendliness.

I tried arranging it alphabetically by name, then alphabetically by category. In either case, I could find no consistency that made sense. My somewhat OCD tendency in this regard meant that I couldn't have stray coupons with no home. For instance, where do you put a coupon for Pillsbury Crescent Rolls? "P" for Pillsbury? "C" for Crescent, or just "B" for Bread? My thought was "P", which was well and good until I went to file the Post Raisin Bran coupon, which obviously should be under "C" for Cereal. So the whole binder became a conundrum, with some items filed by brand name, some by product name, and some by category. And where the heck do you file a coupon for 2 different products, like $1 off the purchase of chicken and cooking crème?

I then realized what is, IMHO, the greatest binder setup ever. In the history of Ever.

We're shopping at primarily one store, right? Why not tailor my binder to that store, so that each aisle of the store is represented by a section of the binder? So the items on Aisle 2 are in Section 2 of the binder. Basically the in-store headers which tell you what is on each aisle also became the category headers of my binder.

I have since used this system for over 2 years and love it. Because I know the store like the back of my hand, I spend no time at all searching for coupons and even filing takes only a few minutes. I don't even need my Table of Contents anymore, I just know that cleaners are on Aisle 8 and deodorant is on Aisle 11!

Then there is the question of the binder itself. I have been through so many that I lost count. I was wasting precious savings on buying binders - finding one that was big enough. With rings strong enough to not open while flipping through, spilling pages everywhere. Finding one that was... well, pretty. I finally found the perfect solution - a heavy duty 3" binder wrapped in a cover from Coupon Clutch. The Clutch has shoulder straps and has thus far lasted almost 2 years, with no signs of wear.

It is widely opined that baseball card holder sheets work great for housing coupons in a binder, and I agree. Fitting 9 different coupons per page, they are the ideal size and make filing and finding a breeze.

Clipping

Clip once per week. Who has time for more anyway? I strongly encourage investing in a heavy-duty paper cutter, the guillotine type (purchased on sale with a coupon, of course). This is especially useful if you have multiple copies of inserts, which you probably do. You can cut like pages together, and all your inserts can be clipped in a matter of minutes. Of course, I suggest only clipping coupons that you might actually use - no point wasting time clipping for an item that you have no intention of purchasing. (Those extra pages can go in a pile to share with friends!)

After clipping the inserts, file immediately into your binder and pull out expired ones in the process.

As a side note on expired coupons... Often members of the military can use coupons up to 6 months after their expiration date. If you feel like sharing, you might enjoy passing them along rather than tossing them.

- - - - - - - - - - - - - - - - - - - ✂ - - - -

Right now, do a little mental checklist of what you've learned so far. You have already learned how to save incredible amounts on your grocery bill, and aside from the few minutes of clipping you haven't committed yourself to any additional time. And that's the point!

Now, armed with a binder full of coupons, you're ready to take on the shopping.

And here is where it all comes together...

Shopping

You're determined to stick to 1-2 stores. You're determined to only buy sale items. You have your binder loaded and ready. What's next?

Consistency and routine. By this point you likely have in mind which store will be the lucky primary recipient of your weekly shopping. Most stores run on a consistent sale cycle, such as Sunday through Saturday, or Wednesday through Tuesday. Find out your store's cycle and shop as near to the beginning of it as possible. Most stores are busiest on weekends, so if that's your only time to shop go early to avoid empty shelves.

It's also helpful to learn whether your store only restocks on certain days. Empty shelves mean you either don't get the item or have to shop a second time, neither of which are productive.

Here's where it becomes obvious that you've made the right choice with your one-store routine:

- You are able to recognize the really good sale prices.
- You're in and out quickly, and never have to waste valuable time looking for an item.
- Because you're a regular, your checkout is more likely to go smoothly (and quickly!)

It is crucial to prepare a list in advance. Again, time is saved by using a shopping tool such as a prepared spreadsheet for calculation. A good spreadsheet, such as the one I have prepared†, will save time by doing your calculations for you. Simply plug in your list and your totals will tally themselves. This is immensely helpful in more ways than one:

- You will know your total before even reaching the cashier.
- A sense of obligation to the pre-planned total will help prevent spontaneous purchases, which are often where we overspend most.
- A portable version allows you to adjust your list on the fly, keeping an accurate running total.

Regardless of what method you use to compile your list, the list itself keeps your spending in check.

Perhaps you're thinking, "How can I prepare a list of sale items if I don't know all that's on sale?" Quite a logical question, I'm glad you asked...

Thanks to the Internet, there is no shortage of information when it comes to sales and coupons. Of course, sorting through it all takes time, which we obviously want to avoid. However, knowing where to look can be an incredible time-saver.

The most dependable source will obviously be your store's own website. Sales are posted in a timely manner and are likely to be accurate. Take a few minutes to look over the online ad when making your list.

There are other sites that match up ads and coupons on a weekly basis, and some of these can be valuable resources. If you decide to rely on such a site for your weekly list, select one that is well-established, comprehensive, and consistently accurate.

With many sale items already on your list, it is no trouble to add any unadvertised deals that you run across while shopping.

The Checkout...

Now your list has been checked off, shopping cart is full, and it's time to head to checkout. Is there any way to ease the pain of checking out with coupons?

First consider why I used the expression "pain of checking out with coupons", and why you instantly knew exactly what I meant...

What makes checkout "painful" at times? Typically, it boils down to clash between cashier and customer. Not necessarily anyone's fault, it can be caused by a number of things, real or perceived:

- The customer's lack of organization.
- The cashier's lack of knowledge about coupon policies.
- The customer's assumption that the cashier will not be helpful.
- The cashier's assumption that the customer is trying to "pull something".
- The customer's incorrect use of coupons.
- The cashier's incorrect understanding of coupons.

The list could go on and on, but you get the point. How can we as couponers do our part to make coupon checkouts everywhere go more smoothly? Never underestimate...

The Power of Honey

Yes, I'm a Georgia Peach and it is perfectly acceptable to call everyone "Honey", but I'm not suggesting you call your cashier such, or that doing so anywhere other than the deep South won't get you slapped silly. No, the Honey I mean is more the "you can catch more flies with *honey* than with vinegar" kind of honey.

Having done my share of time behind a cash register in my 20+ year retail career, I'm sure it comes as no surprise for me to say that there are customers that you *want* to help and those that make it so difficult you'd almost rather they just take their business elsewhere.

See, just as there are cashiers who can make or break our coupon shopping experience, remember that there are couponers that can make or break a cashier's day at work. Just as we have all had one of *those* cashiers, chances are your cashier has had one of *those* couponers. Just as you size up your cashier as you walk up to checkout, she is likely doing the same. And guess what? Just as you sigh with relief at your cashier's friendly smile, she's waiting on that same friendly smile from you. (Of course, cashiers come in all genders, but for simplicity we will refer to them as "she".)

Hence, you can get more flies with honey than with vinegar. Never underestimate the power of kindness. If you are friendly, likeable, and generally easy to deal with, guess who will probably get the benefit of the doubt when the register beeps at your coupon? Whereas, if you are crabby, demanding, or demeaning to the cashier, she's probably looking for a reason to reject your coupon anyway and will welcome the register's beep. And who can blame her?

Speaking of beeps. If you've used more than a coupon or three in different stores, you know that their systems are all set up differently. Some beep at the slightest irregularity, while others will scan virtually anything right on through. It is *your* responsibility as the customer to be sure you are using the coupon correctly. The register is a product of its programming and does not come equipped with a moral agent to detect fraud. Just because it doesn't reject an expired coupon or the purchase of a size other than what is stated does not give one license to commit...

...Coupon Fraud

Whoa, "Fraud"? Such a harsh term! In essence, Coupon Fraud is an attempt to use a coupon for an item that you have not purchased, or to use it in any other manner not in accordance with the terms and conditions printed thereon.

In simple terms: If the coupon says "Not valid on trial size" but you use it on the trial size anyway, that's fraud. If the coupon states it is for a specific product but you use it on a cheaper product of the same manufacturer, that's fraud. If the coupon plainly says "Expires 6/30/12" and you redeem it on 7/1/12, that's fraud. (Unless you are overseas military, who are granted certain exceptions to expiration dates by the manufacturers themselves.)

Many have innocently said, "It's not my fault that the cashiers don't check expiration dates". While partially true, it *is* your fault. And while you might get by with an occasional inaccuracy, when retailers attempt reimbursement for coupons that were not accepted in accordance with plainly written guidelines, they get in trouble themselves. Which makes them (understandably) crack down on coupon acceptance policies. Which, guess what? Makes shopping more difficult for honest couponers.

Here's another myth debunked...

The Customer Is Not Always Right

Seriously. If you work retail, you probably share my hatred for that expression. I firmly believe that that well-intentioned phrase was part of an associate training handbook, in an attempt to teach customer service representatives a mindset that kept their priorities straight. Somewhere along the line a customer got a hold of it and proudly proclaimed, "See! We were right all along!" And thereafter customers of all types chant it as their mantra.

It always amuses me to hear a customer repeat that line to a store employee, as if reminding them of some policy to which they're supposed to adhere. Funny, I've never actually *seen* that posted anywhere.

Can you imagine? A store advertising boldly, "Our Customers Are Always Right!" (which is what we somehow think anyway).

"Yes, sir, I think that 55-in 1080p 3D LED HDTV should be priced at $100."

"Well, umm, sir, we pride ourselves in being the low price leader but we really can't go that low. It is, after all, a $2500 TV."

"But I'm the customer, I'm always right. Your sign says so!"

"You have a point. I'll get it loaded up for you."

It's a ludicrous idea, yet it's usually the first thing a customer says when things aren't going their way.

Reality check: No one is always right. Stores would like our business, but we don't have the "right" to shop there nor the "right" to use coupons. While there may be times that we are absolutely, 100% correct in our interpretation of the meaning of a coupon, ultimately the store does have the right to not accept it. Our understanding of that fact can help us keep the proper perspective and attitude when such a disagreement arises.

- - - - - - - - - - - - - - - - ✂ - - -

To recap, here is your Checkout Code of Conduct:

To Do:
- Before heading to the checkout lane, be sure your coupons are for accurate sizes, quantities, etc.
- Know your store's coupon policies before checking out.
- Choose a normal checkout lane, even if the line is longer.
- Smile.
- Be organized. Have your coupons for checkout ready and in-hand.
- Smile.
- Be considerate of those behind you in line. If you have a large coupon transaction, warn them that you may take longer than usual.
- Thank your cashier for being willing to help you save money.
- Smile.
- If your cashier does an exceptional job, compliment her to the manager and let her know you did so.

To Don't:
- Don't go through the express checkout lane with coupons. It doesn't matter if you only have 8 items – it's not "express" if you are using coupons.

- Don't try to "get by" with using a coupon that you know isn't valid just because you expect the store not to notice.
- Don't assume the customer is always right. No one is always right.
- Don't be demanding, argumentative, or rude. Being right does not excuse being rude.

Now that you're a pro at the shopping trip, you are armed and ready to score some rock bottom bargains for that stockpile!

Speaking of stockpile...

Stockpiling

Often the subject of stockpiling conjures images of basements full of mustard and toothpaste, and hoards of items that couldn't possibly be used by their owners. I have two thoughts on this...

One. I refuse to waste energy worrying about what someone else has in their basement, attic, garage, or under their bed.

Two. Stockpiling does not denote any particular quantity, but rather a practice. And a wise one at that.

By definition, "stockpile" means "a supply stored for future use, usually carefully accrued and maintained." How better to describe the practice of storing extra goods obtained at a cheap price, so as not to pay more for them later?

So, then, how much should you stockpile? Only you can answer this question, for every household is different. A large family will obviously consume more than a couple with no children.

There's no need to over-think the equation, and there's no right or wrong answer. If you find a great deal on toilet paper, get several packs. If you find yourself running out before the next cheap price rolls around, then you know to buy a little more next time. Likewise, if you stock up on free pasta only to find that, 6 months later, you're still buried in pasta, perhaps scale it back a bit next time. And in the meantime, your friends and the local food bank will love the pasta donation.

While not an exact science, sales often run on about a 2-month cycle. Additionally, some items will go on sale with the season, such as baking goods at Thanksgiving, picnic items in early July, and snacks during football season. Most of us are somewhat aware of our family's consumption rate and can plan accordingly.

Also consider the shelf life of an item when deciding how much to purchase. Pay attention to expiration dates when selecting items from the shelves. Items with the closest expiration are usually placed at the front of the shelf for proper inventory rotation, so check toward the back of the shelf for longest life.

As mentioned early on, then, it stands to reason that "stockpiling" simply means purchasing enough to last until you find the next rock-bottom price. For some this may mean a section of the basement or garage set aside, while for others it may simply mean a couple extra pantry shelves.

An established stockpile will make your life so much easier! In addition to the obvious money savings, you will find that having a stockpile...

- Gives you peace of mind, knowing that there's always something for dinner.
- Allows you to be especially frugal during weeks or months where the budget is tight.
- Allows you to share with others if the need arises.
- "Running to the store" takes on a whole new meaning - it probably just means running to the basement to get what you need!

Once you experience the convenience and savings of a stockpile, you'll wonder how you ever kept your sanity without one.

What about Meat & Produce?

Coupons for fresh meat and produce are few and far between, unfortunately. The healthy meals you want to feed your family will need to consist of more than what's to be found on the 'inside aisles' of the store. How can you maximize savings on fresh meat, produce, dairy, and breads?

Fresh Meat and Dairy

The key to saving money on fresh meat and dairy products such as milk consists of 3 components:

- Maximizing the value of sale items
- Enough freezer capacity to stockpile
- Coupons

Maximizing the value of sale items involves more than just watching for a good sale, although that is important too. Most stores mark down meats and milk that are approaching their "sell-by" date. While still perfectly fine, they do need to be prepared or frozen quickly. Familiarize yourself with your store's markdown schedule. Don't be afraid to ask management. Often these deals sell quickly, so shop while markdowns are performed if you can.

Keep in mind that, just as with sales, a markdown doesn't necessarily mean a great deal. Consider the markdowns to be like 'coupons', where the markdown on top of an already good sale price makes for a phenomenal deal. Again, purchase what you can consume and what your freezer space will allow.

Be on the watch for the few coupons that do exist for meat and milk, often what's called a "WYB" coupon. For instance, a coupon might give $1 off fresh chicken WYB a particular seasoning, or a free gallon of milk WYB three cereals. Be careful not to over-pay for the "WYB" items or buy ones that you don't need just to get the discount. Look at the overall cost to be sure it's a deal.

Take the above example of a milk coupon. Cereal can easily cost around $4/box, so at full price your purchase may look like this:

3 boxes cereal @ $4 each:	$12
Free gallon of milk:	$0
Total:	$12

However, on another day with a good cereal sale and coupons, you might snag cereal for $1.50 or less per box. On that day, even without the milk coupon, your total might look like this:

3 boxes cereal @ $1.50 each: $4.50
Milk at full price: $3.50
Total: $8.00

Wow, a whopping $4 difference! The word "Free" is so enticing that it's easy to assume any "free" deal must surely be better. Don't fall victim to great marketing!

Now watch the deal go from Good to Great, using the same aforementioned cereal and milk coupon but combining it with a cereal sale:

3 boxes cereal @ $1.50 each: $4.50
Free milk coupon: $0
Total: $4.50

There's that magic formula again: combining a great sale and a great coupon to maximize savings!

Produce

Stores often mark produce down as well, but obviously fresh veggies that are approaching the end of their shelf lives usually just aren't as appetizing. I mean, a salad made with wilted lettuce is no more appetizing just because it was a bargain, right?

Take advantage of a produce markdown only when you intend to use it right away. $.29/lb ripe bananas are great if you're making fresh banana bread or banana pudding for dinner, but you don't want fruit flies swarming your unused "bargain" 3 days later.

Produce prices are more seasonal than any other in the store, and vary drastically by region. When fruits and veggies are in season in your area, not only are prices cheaper but sales are more common. Adapt your meal preparation to produce that is in season. Make selections carefully, as the freshest produce items with no imperfections will last longer.

Freezing

Many of us may have grown up with mothers who froze fresh veggies from the garden to last through winter, so the thought of freezing to "put back" may not seem practical. However, don't underestimate the power of your freezer to save you money!

One of the best investments in your grocery shopping is plastic freezer bags. There are an abundance of coupons for these, and they go on sale fairly often. Stock up on all sizes.

Consider some of the many items that can be frozen with little or no effort:

Meats

Most of us know that fresh meat can last for a few months in the freezer. Expanding on that though, consider these ideas:

- When you find a great deal on meat, buy extra and freeze.
- Buy bulk packages, which are often cheaper. Divide into smaller, meal-sized portions, and place in freezer bags to freeze. (Be sure to use packaging that is designed for freezer use to prevent freezer burn!
- Use the meat counter services. If a whole pork loin is cheaper than sliced chops of the same cut, buy the whole loin and have the meat counter slice it to your specifications.
- Don't buy pre-pattied burgers, which are usually more expensive and often not of the same quality meat anyway. Buy ground beef at its cheapest price (even having the meat counter grind a roast if it's cheaper). Patty and season the burgers yourself, place wax paper between, and freeze in freezer bags. Frozen patties can be placed directly on the grill or in the pan for a quick meal.

Bread

Most breads can be frozen for a few weeks with little or no effect. If you find a great deal on your favorite bread, don't be afraid to purchase a few extra loaves for the freezer. Bread also thaws very quickly. Frozen slices that are placed out to thaw will be at room temperature within minutes.

When freezing bread, be sure the packaging is as airtight as possible to avoid the accumulation of frost on the bread itself, resulting from trapped humidity in the bag.

Dairy

Many don't think of freezing dairy products, but it's perfectly fine. Almost everything can be frozen. Examples:

- Milk. Yes, milk! Plastic jugs freeze better than cartons. It's a good idea to remove the lid and pour just a bit from the top to allow room for expansion when freezing (which is why the cartons don't do as well). After thawing, shake it up just a bit and you're good to go!
- Cheese. Almost any cheese can be frozen, and does best if unopened. Shredded and sliced cheeses generally do well. Sharper cheeses may tend to be a little more crumbly upon thawing, but are still quite useable. Cheese products such as ricotta, cottage, and spreads generally freeze very well.
- Yogurt. Haven't you ever had frozen yogurt? I rest my case.

Leftovers

Have you ever had just a small amount left over from dinner, and elected to give it to Fido because it didn't seem like enough to bother saving? I keep a number of small freezer containers around, which are perfect for saving those small bites that actually come in quite handy. Got a small serving of corn left over? It may be the perfect amount to add to your next pot of soup! Or perhaps one of the kids doesn't care for the broccoli casserole prepared with the next meal, and the extra serving of corn will be the perfect veggie stand-in.

And wouldn't it be nice to have a home-cooked meal after a long day at work? On occasion, if you're preparing a time-consuming dish anyway, double the recipe and freeze the other half. For instance, our family loves lasagna. It doesn't take much extra time to prepare two dishes vs. one, and the extra uncooked dish goes into the freezer to be cooked later. It is such a stress-reliever to have a small handful of such dishes to choose from in a pinch.

Do you have older kids that stay at home by themselves some? Serving-size portions of their favorite meals in the freezer make great after-school snacks or lunches during the summer, and are certainly much cheaper and healthier than their microwaveable store-bought counterparts!

Common Mistakes

I'm an expert on this subject, as I have made my share of mistakes. When it comes to coupon shopping and stockpiling, I unfortunately learned a few things the hard way.

Allow me to save you the trouble by covering some of the most common couponing mistakes.

Overspending

Say what? How can one overspend when using coupons? Very easily, actually. You see, saving money is addicting. The rush of seeing your total drop to almost nothing is a thrill that you will want to repeat again and again. It becomes tempting to purchase items that you don't really even need and probably won't use, simply because they are cheap and will give you that thrill.

Buying Too Much

Hand in hand with overspending, this applies to purchasing more of an item then will actually be used, resulting in waste. Remember that any amount spent on a wasted item, no matter how little, is too much.

Impatience

Just because an item is on sale, does not mean it's a *great* sale. Know your prices, and have the patience to wait on that really good deal before stocking up.

Obsession

I admit, I'm obsessed with savings. A level of obsession might actually be healthy, if it means that you are always conscientious of keeping expenditures to a minimum. However, an unhealthy obsession leads to stress and worry that you might have missed a deal. That level of obsession will make you want to drive across town to snag free toothpaste, or make several stops on the way home from work rather than spend the evening with your family and preserve your sanity.

I have to admit - because I was on TV, run a successful coupon website, teach classes, and so on, others often assume that I am aware of every deal out there at any given time. I am often asked if I got the latest deal at the local drug store, and the fact that I wasn't even aware of the deal seems to come as a shock to some. However, we save an average of about 80% on groceries. With that number, I just don't feel like we're missing out on anything!

Is there room for improvement? Perhaps, and always looking for that room is part of the whole point. Finding the perfect balance between savings accomplished and time spent doing so is the ultimate goal. Because your sanity is part of the success equation, when you have found that perfect balance give yourself a great big pat on the back and keep up the good work!

References

*WMC Family Budget
The comprehensive budget spreadsheet, detailing monthly and annual expenditures and automatically totaling by category and payee, while comparing to budgeted totals. Available for download at www.workingmomcoupons.com.

**Manufacturer Contact List
The most complete list of manufacturer contacts on the web! This free download shows complete contact information for all major household grocery manufacturers, as well as their likelihood to send coupons upon request and links to existing printable coupons online. Also available for download at www.workingmomcoupons.com.

†WMC Couponing Spreadsheet
The all-in-one couponing tool that I use to keep shopping simple and structured. Use on your personal computer or portable device. Available in Excel and Numbers formats at www.workingmomcoupons.com.